What Was the Holocaust?

by Gail Herman

illustrated by Jerry Hoare

Penguin Workshop
An Imprint of Penguin Random House

To Our Readers

This book is about an event in history that is so terrible, it seems almost impossible to believe it actually happened. But it did. The Holocaust refers to the murder of twelve million people in Europe. Six million of them were Jewish. It didn't happen all that long ago—from 1939 to the middle of 1945.

After you finish reading this book, you will know who planned the Holocaust, where and when it took place, and how it was carried out. But one thing you won't learn is why it happened. That's because there really is no way to explain something that is so purely evil.

For a long time we thought about whether or not to publish a book about the Holocaust. We wondered if the subject was too awful for young readers. But we decided it was such an important event that not including the Holocaust in the series would be wrong. The few survivors of the Holocaust are very old now. When they are no longer alive, it will be up to books to tell the painful story of what happened. Very likely you will have lots of questions after you finish reading this. We hope you turn to your family or your teachers to talk about them.

Jane O'Connor
Jane O'Connor, Editor

Over the past ten years, I have been teaching young people the important lessons of the Holocaust as well as educating teachers on methods to use to introduce this topic. I have searched for a book like *What Was the Holocaust?* but found nothing until now.

This book will help upper-elementary and early-middle-school-age students begin to understand the complexities of the topic. In a well thought out and meaningful way, the author delves into the rise of the Nazi Party, ghettos, concentration camps, resistance, and heroes.

I have found that so many students connect deeply to this story of destruction and survival, and yearn to know about it. *What Was the Holocaust?* fills that need; it is a fantastic source that will help shape a young person's understanding of this dark period in time.

Ilyse Shainbrown
M.A. Holocaust and Genocide Studies
Holocaust educator

For my parents, and the men and women
of their generation—GH

PENGUIN WORKSHOP
Penguin Young Readers Group
An Imprint of Penguin Random House LLC

Copyright © 2018 by Penguin Random House LLC. All rights reserved. Published by Penguin Workshop, an imprint of Penguin Random House LLC, 345 Hudson Street, New York, New York 10014. PENGUIN and PENGUIN WORKSHOP are trademarks of Penguin Books Ltd. WHO HQ & Design is a registered trademark of Penguin Random House LLC. Printed in the USA.

Library of Congress Cataloging-in-Publication Data is available.

ISBN 9780451533906 (paperback)   10 9 8 7 6 5 4 3
ISBN 9780451533920 (library binding)   10 9 8 7 6 5 4 3 2

Contents

What Was the Holocaust? 1

Anti-Semitism 8

Adolf Hitler 12

The Nazis 17

Hitler in Power 29

War! 36

In the Ghetto 46

Life in the Concentration Camps 56

The Final Solution 64

Fighting Back 77

Freedom! 86

After 92

Timelines 104

Bibliography 106

What Was the Holocaust?

**May 1945: Volary, a small town in what
is now the Czech Republic**

Gerda Weissmann stood outside an old bicycle factory. She weighed sixty-five pounds. Her hair was white, although she was not even twenty-one.

Inside the empty building, dozens of women lay on straw. Most were sick. Many were dying. Like Gerda, they were all Jewish. For many years they had suffered under the rule of Nazi Germany.

For Gerda, the horror had begun six years earlier.

It was late summer. She was fifteen years old. And she had just come home from vacation. On September 1, 1939, the weather was glorious, the sky a bright blue. Suddenly, German airplanes blocked the sun. They roared over Gerda's home in Bielsko, Poland. Tanks rolled down the streets. The German army was invading Poland.

It was the start of World War II, which lasted in Europe until May of 1945.

Many local people waved Nazi flags. They cheered for their new leader, Adolf Hitler. They were glad Hitler had taken over Poland. Hitler hoped to take over all of Europe.

The Jews of Bielsko were not happy at all. They knew of the Nazis' hatred for Jews.

Gerda and her family were told to leave their home so local German-Poles could move in. Gerda's garden was fenced off with a sign that read: "No dogs or Jews allowed." They lived in a basement, with no water or electricity.

After a while, all Jews in Bielsko were rounded up. Trucks took them to different prison camps. Gerda was separated from her mother. She never saw her again. She never saw anybody else in her family again, either. Through the rest of the war, Gerda was moved from one concentration camp to another. She labored in Nazi-run factories. She hauled coal onto trains. By 1945, she was half-dead.

And yet Gerda was one of the more fortunate ones. She survived.

Six million Jews did not. They were killed by the Nazis in concentration camps. About six million other victims were also led to their deaths: gay people, the Roma, disabled people, and people from certain religious and political groups.

That day in 1945 at the factory, Gerda saw a car approach. Two men—United States soldiers—jumped out. One came over. He was big and strong. To Gerda, he looked like a god.

"Does anybody here speak German or English?" he asked in German.

"I speak German," Gerda answered. Then she added, "We are Jewish, you know."

"So am I," the man said. His name was Kurt Klein. "May I see the other ladies?" he added. Then the man held the door for Gerda to go inside the factory. It was a simple, polite thing to do. But it made her feel human again.

One year later, Gerda and Kurt Klein were married.

Gerda Weissmann's wartime story ended on a note of hope. That was rare for the millions who suffered during the Holocaust.

The word *holocaust*—rooted in Greek—means a "sacrifice by fire." But it also means any great destruction and loss of life.

From 1939 to 1945, all across Europe, Jews and people from other groups were murdered simply because of who they were.

How did this happen?

CHAPTER 1
Anti-Semitism

Anti-Semitism is the hatred of Jews. It goes back thousands of years to ancient Rome.

When Christianity took hold in the world, anti-Jewish feeling spread. There were false, awful stories that Jews had killed Jesus. They were blamed for causing disease and for bad crops. Sometimes this led to violent attacks against Jews. Sometimes anti-Jewish laws were passed: In certain parts of Europe, Jews couldn't own land. They could not be citizens.

In more modern times, around the 1800s, countries in Europe developed fairer laws. Life opened up for Jewish people. They had more freedom. Some Jews kept their old customs. Some did not. More and more, Jews considered themselves German . . . or Austrian . . . or French . . . before they thought of themselves as Jewish.

Then, in 1914, the kaiser (emperor) of Germany started a world war in Europe. It raged on until 1918 with Germany's surrender. A treaty was signed with very harsh terms for Germany. The kaiser was gone. Germany lost land. It had to disband its army. For starting the war, it had to pay billions of dollars to the countries that Germany had fought against. But Germany didn't have any money.

As in the past, much of the blame for Germany's woes fell on the Jews. In 1919, Germany tried to set up a democracy. The group of elected representatives was called the Reichstag. A president was elected,

Germans protesting
the peace treaty signed
after World War I

too. The president, in turn, chose a chancellor. The chancellor held a lot of power. But he still had to answer to the president and the Reichstag.

This new government was supposed to offer a better future for Germany. But it faced big challenges. For example, how would Germany pay all the money it owed? The government thought the answer was to print money. More and more money.

Soon there were so many German dollars—marks—they became almost worthless. Prices went up day by day, hour by hour. One man bought a cup of coffee for 5,000 marks, already a very high price. When he ordered a second cup, the price had shot up to 9,000 marks! People carried cash around in wheelbarrows.

By 1929, millions of Germans were out of work. Most had their savings wiped out. Many wanted change, a new direction for the country.

But who could lead the country to a new and better future?

Germans turned to the worst person possible— Adolf Hitler.

CHAPTER 2
Adolf Hitler

When Adolf Hitler was a boy, no one expected much of him. He was born on April 20, 1889, in a small town in Austria called Braunau am Inn. It bordered Germany, and the people there spoke German. Hitler's family wasn't rich. But they did fine.

Hitler's father was a harsh man, strict and quick to punish. He wanted his son to work in government. But Hitler wasn't interested. He wanted to be an artist.

Hitler had always been a lazy student, but after his father's death, he started failing classes. A few years later, he dropped out of school. He knew his mother would support him. She had always spoiled him. So he didn't do much of anything. He just daydreamed.

In 1907, Hitler was turned down by an art school. At the end of the year, his mother died.

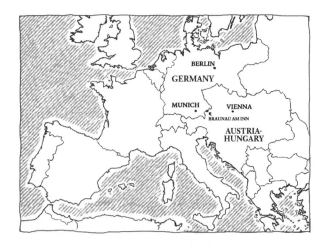

With nothing keeping him at home, he moved to Austria's capital, Vienna. Once again, he lounged around, talking in cafés about politics, art, and ideas.

Vienna had a large Jewish community. But the city was known for its anti-Semitism. Anti-Jewish newspapers and pamphlets were sold everywhere. Hitler read them all. The mayor spoke out against Jews, too. Later Hitler would say that Vienna was where his ideas came together.

Time passed. Hitler had no job. He sold his belongings and slept on park benches. Finally he settled into a home for poor men, scraping by, selling his artwork. A failure, known for fits of temper, Hitler was homeless and friendless. He left Vienna in 1913.

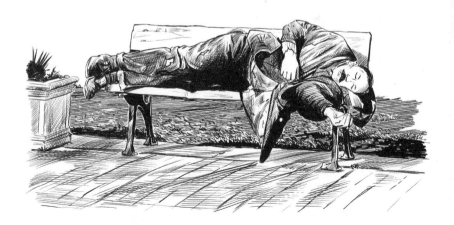

Hitler had always felt that Germany held more promise for him than Austria. So he moved to the German city of Munich. When World War I broke out, he signed up to fight for the German army. In the army, Hitler finally found success. He won medals for bravery. When Germany surrendered, Hitler was crushed. Like so many others, he blamed Jews for the defeat.

And he was ready to do something about it.

CHAPTER 3
The Nazis

In 1919, Adolf Hitler went to a meeting in Munich. It was held by a new political group— the German Workers' Party. About twenty-five people were there. In fact, the whole political party had only about fifty members.

The party wanted a strong, proud Germany. And they blamed Jews for all the country's problems. This appealed to Hitler. He didn't believe that the Jews of Germany were "real" Germans. He considered them "sub-human." True Germans belonged to what the party called the "Aryan" race. The ideal Aryan had blond hair and blue eyes. Of course, some Jews had blond hair and blue eyes, while Hitler himself had brown hair and brown eyes. But that didn't make any difference to him: Jews weren't Aryans, and he was.

Hitler joined the German Workers' Party. He rose up the ranks. He gave spellbinding speeches. He knew what people wanted to hear and how to work up a crowd. Did people feel betrayed by the new government? Yes! Were they worried about jobs? Yes! Could Germany be great again? Yes! In one short year, the party grew to three thousand members. And Hitler was its leader.

Hitler chose the swastika, a hooked cross, for the party's symbol. It was an image used in Indian religions. But that is not why he chose it. Some people believed that thousands of years ago, Aryan nomads had used this same symbol. So to Hitler, the swastika represented the Aryan race.

Hitler also added two words to the party name: National Socialist. In German, the name was abbreviated to the NSDAP, then shortened even more. It was just known as the Nazi Party.

As Nazi leader, Hitler saw two main problems: Germany needed to be bigger and stronger. And something had to be done about the Jews.

In 1923, Hitler began his grab for power. On November 8, he went to a Munich beer hall. He brought along storm troopers—armed Nazis known for violence. German government officials were holding a meeting. He wanted to overthrow these leaders, then march to Berlin, the nation's capital.

At 8:30 p.m., Hitler fired a pistol at the ceiling. With the storm troopers' help, the officials were taken prisoner. But then things fell apart. There were gunshots. People were killed. Hitler was arrested.

His trial lasted almost a month. It was big

news. In court, Hitler lashed out at the Jews. He spoke about German pride. He was sent to jail. But the trial drew even more people to the party and to Hitler.

While he was in prison, Hitler entertained visitors. He feasted on wine and chocolate. And he wrote a book called *Mein Kampf*, which means "My Struggle." What did he struggle against? The Jewish "race." He accused Jews of plotting to take over the world.

Mein Kampf

During the time the Nazis were in power, millions of copies of *Mein Kampf* were sold. But after World War II, the German government banned it, to block Hitler's hateful message. Today a new edition is out with side notes and explanations. Will the book show readers how evil Hitler was? Or bring new fans to his terrible ideas?

When Hitler left prison, the Nazis were more powerful than ever. They held big parades. They staged rallies. Storm troopers and a special new military group—the SS—marched in crisp new uniforms.

Many Germans wanted a hero—someone to rescue them from hard times. Their mistake was turning to Adolf Hitler to be their new leader.

Hitler decided to run for president. He ran against President Paul von Hindenburg. It was a close election. But Hitler lost. Reichstag elections were held. No party had a major victory. Instead the government was made up of many small groups. Each one worked against

Paul von Hindenburg

the others. The government came to a standstill.

President von Hindenburg needed the support of the Nazis. With his own party as well as Hitler's Nazis behind him, he'd have enough power to govern. So von Hindenburg appointed Hitler chancellor.

At noon, January 30, 1933, Hitler was sworn in. By that night, thousands lined the streets to watch the SS parade through Berlin. Its officers marched in step, carrying torches and singing. At the president's palace, Hitler stood at the window. A spotlight cast him in a bright glow. Everyone in

the crowd raised their arms in the Nazi salute.

One newscaster said, "Nothing like this has ever been seen before."

German radio broadcast the event. In Jewish homes, families listened, knowing trouble was in store.

There were only about 523,000 Jews out of Germany's 67 million people. That year, about 37,000 emigrated. They left the country to start a new life.

Others stayed. Some didn't have the money to leave. Others didn't want to. Germany was their home. They told themselves that Jews had gone through bad times before. And in the recent past, life had improved. Now Jews were German citizens with full rights. They didn't believe anything terrible would happen. Soon Hitler would fade away. Besides, he was not the real German leader. There was still von Hindenburg and the Reichstag.

For now.

CHAPTER 4
Hitler in Power

One month later, the Reichstag building was set on fire. Hitler blamed his political enemies. He had thousands arrested. They were tortured and thrown into a special prison. It was outside Munich in a town called Dachau. It was the first of the Nazi concentration camps—prisons where people were "concentrated" in great numbers under brutal conditions. For Hitler, however, jailing political criminals was not enough.

President von Hindenburg was old and frail by then and agreed to give the chancellor—Adolf Hitler—full power. In the next few months, Hitler made all political parties illegal except his own—the Nazis. From then on, he didn't need approval from the president or the Reichstag to do what he wanted.

Hitler was free to decide what to do about the Jews.

His first step was to separate them from the rest of society. By doing this, he believed they'd leave Germany once and for all. Hitler began to pass anti-Jewish laws. First he focused on schools.

Students had to say "Heil Hitler" (Hail Hitler) when they arrived, at the start of each class, and at the end of the day. Textbooks were rewritten—every subject needed to praise Hitler and Germany and put down Jews. If teachers didn't teach Nazi beliefs about the Aryan race, they were fired. Soon there could only be a certain number of Jewish students in public schools. Those students had to sit in the last row.

And this was just the beginning.

Hitler Youth

Hitler thought young Aryans were the future of Germany. He founded the Hitler Youth in the early 1920s—Jews and other "sub-humans" were not allowed. Boys trained to be storm troopers, and girls learned to be good wives and mothers. By 1939, membership was no longer a choice. Boys hiked, camped, and played sports. They practiced marching and shooting, and starting up fights against Jews. Girls ran, swam, and learned to cook. Hitler Youth held large colorful rallies, and the group stayed loyal to Hitler to the end of World War II.

President von Hindenburg died the next year (1934). In short order, Hitler combined von Hindenburg's job with his own. There was no longer a president and a chancellor. There was only Hitler. On August 2, 1934, he named himself führer (say: FYUR-er), which means "leader" in German.

More concentration camps were built. Political opponents were jailed without trials. In 1935, other groups were imprisoned, including gay people.

More anti-Jewish laws were passed, too. But Hitler was careful. He didn't pass all the laws at once. He tested the mood of the country, announcing just a few laws at a time. When non-Jewish citizens didn't object, he took away more rights from the Jews.

In the beginning, Jews couldn't hold certain jobs. They couldn't work for the government. Or practice law or medicine, or teach in public schools. Jewish professors were kicked off the faculty of universities.

Then more laws passed: Jews couldn't marry non-Jews. They had to carry Jewish ID cards. Their stores and homes had to be marked with a Jewish star. Soon they were no longer German citizens.

New laws passed almost every month. Jews couldn't own businesses or property. They couldn't go to parks or movies or play sports with non-Jews. In time, they had to wear a badge with a yellow star on their clothes everywhere they went.

For Jews, it was like a noose being pulled tighter and tighter.

CHAPTER 5
War!

Other countries watched Hitler gain power and saw what the Nazis were doing to the Jewish people. But they took no action. So Hitler went further. He ignored the World War I treaty. He put an army together. In March 1938, Nazi troops marched into neighboring Austria. Hitler rode behind them. He was met by cheering crowds.

Most Austrians were eager to be part of what Hitler called the Third Reich—Germany's new empire that soon would rule the world and last a thousand years. The Austrians didn't mind harsh anti-Jewish laws going into effect. Almost immediately, Jews were attacked on the streets.

That September, Hitler demanded that the Sudetenland, a Czech region, become part of the Reich, too. Many Germans lived there. So it was only right, Hitler said. If he didn't get the land, he threatened war. To avoid conflict, Great Britain agreed, and other countries followed.

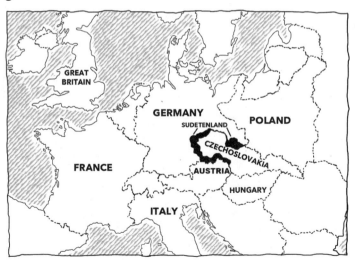

Germany was growing stronger and bigger. And as time passed, restrictions against Jews grew stronger, too. On November 9, 1938, anti-Jewish violence swept across Germany and Austria.

During Kristallnacht (the "Night of Broken

Glass"), more than 7,000 Jewish businesses were destroyed, along with 267 synagogues. Shattered glass from windows lined the streets. Ninety-one Jews were killed.

Afterward, the Jewish community received a bill for damages—damages done by the Nazis. Hundreds of thousands of Jewish men were arrested. They were sent to concentration camps, the first to be imprisoned just for being Jews.

Now the Nazis were sure that no Jews would want to remain in the Reich. And indeed, by the end of the 1930s, more than half the Jewish population fled to other European countries, to the United States, and to Palestine. But many couldn't leave. Some simply didn't have the money. Also, other countries had set limits on how many Jewish immigrants could enter. That was because in America and in Europe, millions of people were out of work. So countries didn't want immigrants arriving and competing for the few jobs that were there.

US Immigration

In the United States, there was also strong anti-Semitism. And although President Franklin D. Roosevelt had many Jewish advisors in his government, the mood of the country was against taking in Jewish immigrants. When the *St. Louis*, a ship carrying nine hundred German-Jewish passengers, wanted to dock on the Florida coast, it was sent back to Europe. Eventually more than 250 of its passengers were killed in the Holocaust.

After Hitler seized the Czech capital city of Prague in March of 1939, European leaders finally took a stand. They said Germany had to stop its conquests.

Hitler didn't listen. On September 1, he invaded Poland. Two days later, Great Britain and France declared war against the Third

Reich. It was the start of World War II.

Once Germany took over Poland, anti-Jewish laws went into effect there. In addition, thousands of Poles were forced to leave their homes, to make way for German settlers. Many Poles were sent to camps where they did hard labor or were killed.

In the spring, Hitler invaded Denmark, Norway, the Netherlands, Belgium, and France. In April 1941, he took over Yugoslavia and Greece; then in June, Nazi troops marched into the Soviet Union. Hitler was truly creating an empire.

We are heroes, Hitler told the German people. We are the master race.

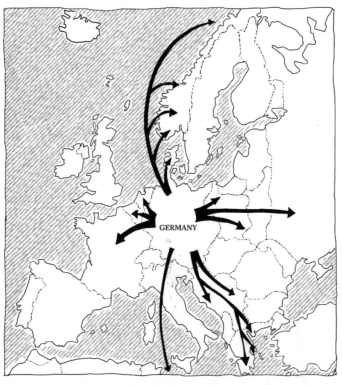

Arrows show where German troops invaded

The Two Sides in World War II

Two groups of countries fought each other in the Second World War (1939–1945). The Axis powers—Germany, Italy, and Japan—was one group. Its goal was German rule in Europe, Italian rule around the Mediterranean Sea, and Japanese rule in the Far Eastern part of the world. The other group—the Allies—was led by Great Britain and the Soviet Union.

The United States hoped to stay out of the war. But it joined the Allies after Japan bombed Pearl Harbor, a US Navy base in Hawaii, in December of 1941. The Allies' goal was to defeat the Axis powers, but it took four more years for that to happen.

CHAPTER 6
In the Ghetto

For Hitler, a new problem came with these victories. There were many Jews in the countries he invaded. Poland alone had 3.3 million Jewish people. What could be done with them?

Hitler decided to force Jews to live in separate areas of cities and towns. Just months after the Polish invasion, the first ghettos were created. Before the war's end, there were at least a thousand ghettos in German-occupied countries.

The term *ghetto* goes back centuries. In the past, it had meant the part of a city where Jews were forced to live. During the Third Reich, the ghettos set up by the Nazis were always in the poorest part of a town and never large enough for all the Jews living in them. The Warsaw ghetto took up only sixteen city blocks, yet at one point it housed almost half a million people. Even so, at first, many Jews thought ghettos weren't such a bad idea. They hoped it might be better to have their own little area, free from Nazi attacks.

That proved not to be true.

The first and biggest ghettos were in Poland: in Lodz and Warsaw. Ghettos were later set up across eastern Europe. Thousands and thousands of Jews from across the Reich were sent to the larger ones. Some ghettos were small towns with roads closed off. Others were walled-in spaces in cities.

Workers build a wall to close off a ghetto

Non-Jews had to move out. Jews had to move in. Jewish councils were selected for running the day-to-day business of the ghettos.

The mayor of one town described families moving into the ghetto, trudging silently through the snow. He wrote that there was "a vast crowd of wandering people. The aged were helped by children. There were women with infants in their arms. All had bundles ... blankets, clothing, rags."

Once all the Jews were inside, the ghetto was sealed. It was closed off from the world, with high walls, barbed wire, and guarded gates. Except for a few Jewish workers—those carting garbage or digging ditches, for instance—no one was allowed to leave. The penalty for escape was death. "If you went too close to the fence, you just got shot," one survivor explained.

The Jews were cut off in other ways, too. Printing presses, radios, and telephones were taken away. They couldn't learn what was going on in the outside world, or tell anyone about their plight.

In the beginning, many residents still had money and food. They tried to make ghetto life seem as normal as possible. For instance, cafés opened in the Warsaw ghetto. Watchmakers and tailors set up shops. Children went to school. But as time wore on, life got worse.

There were Nazi-run factories in the Lodz and Warsaw ghettos where Jews were forced to make guns and uniforms for Hitler's troops. Schools were closed, so students had to meet in secret. If Nazi officials appeared, the boys and girls quickly hid their books.

At any time, Nazis could come into the ghetto and seize men right off the streets. They'd make them build roads or new concentration camps. And sometimes, the men wouldn't come back. They ended up in the prison camps they helped build.

Fuel and food became scarce. At one point in the Warsaw ghetto, Nazis limited Jews to 180 calories' worth of food each day. That's about the same number of calories as in one bowl of cereal.

Over time, more and more Jews were brought to the Warsaw ghetto—from Berlin, from Vienna, from every corner of the Third Reich. With little heat, food, or running water, people began to die.

By spring of 1941, between five and six thousand people were dying each month in the Warsaw ghetto. Carts collected bodies from the streets every morning.

How could people hope to survive?

Some planted vegetable gardens.

Some smuggled in food. Small children could squeeze through cracks in the wall. Others would wait for Nazi guards to turn away, then they'd race through the gate to the outside world. There, they'd exchange money or goods for food. They'd hide the bread or potatoes in their clothes. When it seemed safe, they'd hurry back into the ghetto.

Smuggling was a form of resistance. Resistance meant standing up to the Nazis, fighting back. Resistance groups sprang up in many ghettos. In the Warsaw and Lodz ghettos, young men and women traveled back and forth through underground sewer tunnels to spread the news of what was happening.

It seemed no one cared what was being done to the Jews.

For children, ghetto life was especially harsh.

There were no parks, no trees. Every day they were hungry. Every day they lived in fear. Would a father or mother, sister or brother, be taken away?

People struggled to hold on to their religion and take strength from it. When one boy in Lodz named Chaim turned thirteen, his parents celebrated with a bar mitzvah, an important Jewish ceremony. They gave him half a loaf of bread as a present.

"I couldn't even imagine for how long they saved it from themselves," he said later.

He cried as he ate.

CHAPTER 7
Life in the Concentration Camps

As time went on, hundreds more concentration camps were built for prisoners of the Nazis.

At every camp, as soon as prisoners arrived, men and older boys were separated from women and older girls. Generally, young children weren't held in these camps. They were too small to work. Often, they were left behind in towns or ghettos—basically orphaned.

Once inside, prisoners were given a striped uniform: Men wore a jacket, pants, cap, and wooden shoes. Women were given striped skirts and tops.

Every prisoner had a number. No names were ever used. At Auschwitz and some other camps, the number was tattooed onto a prisoner's arm.

Next, everyone's heads were shaved. "We all looked alike," said one survivor. "Rich, poor, young, old. We shared the same fate . . ."

The Nazis did this for two reasons. They wanted to make prisoners feel less than human. They also used the hair to make cloth and thread for uniforms and other items.

All prisoners had to work. Those sent to coal mines lasted only about a month. They died from sickness and exhaustion. In factories, if Nazi guards thought the prisoners were working too slowly, they shot them.

Every camp had a Nazi commander. At the Plaszow camp in Poland, Amon Goeth was said to shoot Jews for sport from his balcony. Otto Riemer, at Mauthausen in Austria, gave cigarettes and extra vacation time to guards who killed the most prisoners.

All camps had terrible conditions. Bunk beds were stacked side by side, one on top of the other, with two or three to a bed, sometimes more. Hundreds of prisoners used one bathroom with only a few faucets. Toilets were long slabs of wood or concrete, with dozens of holes cut out for seats. Prisoners had no clean water or soap or changes of clothes.

Usually, prisoners woke at 4:00 a.m. Breakfast was watery soup, coffee, and a piece of bread. After, everyone lined up for roll call. Thousands of prisoners stood outside in rows. It took hours. In Poland, winter temperatures were always below freezing. If prisoners had died during the night, their bodies were brought outside, too. Everyone needed to be counted.

Next, the prisoners went off in work teams. In some camps, prison orchestras played music as the workers marched outside. Many camps had a sign that read "Work will set you free." Nothing was further from the truth.

At the quarry, mine, or construction site, workers had to run as they carried heavy loads. Otherwise, they would be shot. There was a lunch break: soup again. After twelve to fourteen hours, they marched back to camp. Then came evening roll call, followed by soup. The next day it started all over again.

In spite of how they were treated, prisoners tried to keep some sense of their own dignity and humanity. Some wrote stories and poems. They painted and drew. Some even held religious ceremonies in secret. Still, their old lives seemed like an impossible dream.

CHAPTER 8
The Final Solution

In June 1941, German troops crossed into the Soviet Union. About four million Jews lived in the region. Now came a new order: Don't bother sending Jews to camps or ghettos. Kill them right away. This was the next step in Hitler's plan. Special vans followed the German army from town to town. The Nazis forced Jews into them, then piped poisonous gas into the back.

Outside the city of Kiev at Babi Yar, thirty-three thousand Jews were killed in two days. They were lined up in small groups along the edge of a ravine. Then they were shot, their bodies falling onto the dead below.

Within eighteen months, one million people were killed. Even so, Hitler wanted better, faster

methods of murder. He decided on something called the Final Solution, a top secret plan to completely wipe out the Jews in death camps all over Poland.

The Wannsee Conference

Outside of Berlin at Wannsee, a conference was held on January 20, 1942. It brought together top Nazi officials to learn about the plan for the Final Solution. The men discussed methods of mass murder. A poisonous gas called Zyklon B was to be used. They also talked over transportation issues—how to get all the Jews in occupied Europe to death camps. They decided Jews would be rounded up and taken by train.

All the officials at Wannsee gave their approval to the Final Solution.

Zyklon B pellets

Poland became the land of death camps. The first was in Chelmno. It went into operation in December of 1941. Three others were quickly built: Belzec, Sobibor, and Treblinka, with huge gas chambers. More than a thousand people could be killed at a time. Gas chambers were added to the concentration camp at Majdanek, and built in other camps as well.

The biggest camp was the one at Auschwitz. Even before the gas chambers were built, Auschwitz had been a huge complex. It had more than forty sub-camps. One sub-camp alone held ten thousand inmates. It had factories, farms, and coal mines. At Auschwitz, ID numbers were tattooed on prisoners' arms. In the end, more than one million people died there. The vast majority of victims were Jewish.

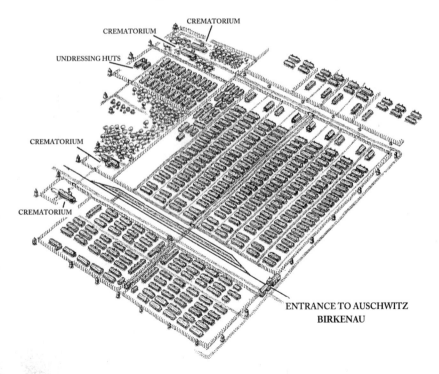

CREMATORIUM
CREMATORIUM
UNDRESSING HUTS
CREMATORIUM
CREMATORIUM
ENTRANCE TO AUSCHWITZ BIRKENAU

Hitler ordered all the ghettos emptied. In the Lodz ghetto, the first major "roundups"—mass arrests—took place in early 1942. In September, another order was issued. The SS wanted twenty-five thousand more people, including children. Parents refused. So the Nazis declared a twenty-four-hour curfew. No one could go outside for eight days. During that time, the SS searched apartment after apartment. If anyone resisted, they were shot. In the end, around fifteen thousand people were seized. At the nearby station, a train waited. It was only thirty miles from Lodz to the camp at Chelmno.

Anne Frank (1929–1945)

Anne Frank was a young Jewish girl born in Germany. When she was four, her family moved to Amsterdam to escape the Nazis. Seven years later, Hitler invaded the Netherlands. In July 1942, the Frank family went into hiding. They lived in a secret part of a building that housed Anne's father's company. For more than two years, the Franks shared the space

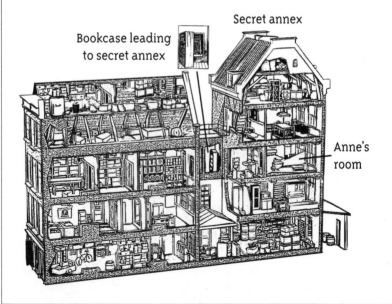

Bookcase leading to secret annex

Secret annex

Anne's room

with another family and a friend. They were unable to go outside, talk loudly, or open curtains.

Anne recorded her story—her feelings, fears, hopes, and dreams—in a diary. In August of 1944, the group was discovered and arrested. Anne and her sister both died in a concentration camp, just weeks before the war ended. Anne was fifteen. But she lives on in her diary, which was found by a family friend. It's been translated into sixty-seven languages and is read throughout the world.

Death camps were located near railway lines so when prisoners got off trains, they didn't have far to go. Transit camps were also set up—one outside Paris, another outside Amsterdam, and one in Belgium. Jews would be arrested, gathered in transit camps, then sent on to Poland and death.

People lived in constant fear of these roundups.

They usually began at dawn, with a loud knock. Officers burst into an apartment. People were sleepy and confused, and very scared. The officers searched every closet, every cabinet, to make sure they found everyone. They gave people minutes to pack before starting on a journey that would end at the death camps in Poland.

Some train cars had open tops, some closed. Some were cattle cars, used to move herds of cows. Each car was freezing cold in winter, boiling hot in summer.

Closed cattle cars were the worst. There were no windows. People rode in total darkness, eighty to one hundred prisoners packed into a space about the size of four elevators. They had no water or food. There was no bathroom, just a bucket.

Some journeys took days. By the time the train reached the camp, many had already died. When the train doors opened, people thought: At last! Fresh air!

Then they saw the camp. The prison complex with dark gloomy buildings. Guard towers and electric fences. Machine guns. Searchlights. SS officers with whips and rifles. Vicious dogs.

Gerda Weissmann Klein speaking at the US Holocaust Memorial Museum

The Reichstag building in Berlin, Germany, 1930

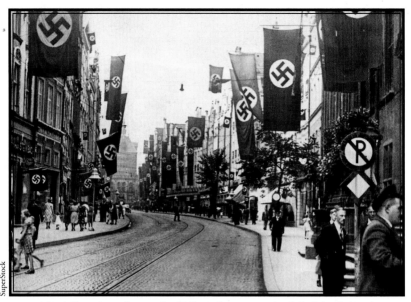

Nazi flags hanging on buildings in a street in Gdańsk, Poland

1930s portrait of Adolf Hitler in his military
uniform wearing a swastika armband

Adolf Hitler and German president
Paul von Hindenburg in Berlin, Germany, 1934

Hitler Youth in front of the town hall in
Tomaszów Mazowiecki, Poland, May 1941

Jewish refugee children waving at the Statue of Liberty from
the deck of the ocean liner *President Harding* in 1939

German-Jewish refugees aboard the *St. Louis* ocean liner arrive in
Antwerp, Belgium, after not being allowed to dock in the United States

Adolf Hitler at the Bückeberg Harvest Festival
in Germany on October 1, 1934

Arrival of a train bringing Hungarian Jews to Auschwitz in Poland, circa 1942

Men building a brick wall around the Warsaw ghetto in 1939

Ira Nowinski/Corbis/VCG

Gateway to the Auschwitz concentration camp

amon toussia-cohen/Getty Images

Barbed wire fence at Auschwitz

Women in the barracks at Auschwitz, January 1945

Children in Auschwitz, 1945

A portrait of Anne Frank from her own photo album, May 1942

Oskar Schindler in Israel in 1962

Russian soldiers liberating
Auschwitz, 1945

Nazi leaders accused of wartime atrocities listen to proceedings
at the trials in Nuremberg, Germany, 1946

The judges' bench in the Nuremberg trials, 1946

At Auschwitz, SS doctors waited for the prisoners. These doctors decided each prisoner's fate in a "selection." The strongest went to a labor camp. Those who couldn't work were sent right away to their deaths. SS officers told these people they were going to take showers, to wash off the dust from the long trip. They led groups to a giant room to undress. Sometimes, an officer gave out soap and towels. But this was all a trick.

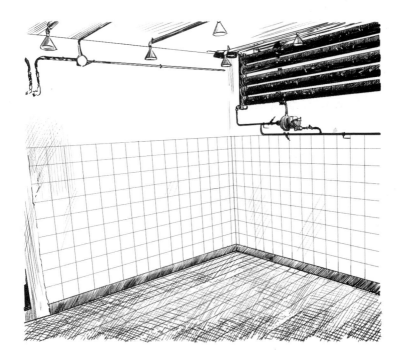

The door to another room opened. Prisoners saw showerheads. When they stepped inside, the door was sealed tight. No water came down. Instead, poison gas was piped in. The "shower room" was a death chamber. Everyone died in minutes. Afterward the bodies were cremated—burned to ash—in ovens.

At first, the Allies didn't believe these death camps really existed. But the news spread. World leaders, however, didn't act. The best plan, the Allies reasoned, was to end the war as quickly as possible. And then the Jews would be helped, too. But the war lasted until 1945. At that point twelve million people, half of them Jewish, had been murdered.

CHAPTER 9
Fighting Back

Jews knew the truth about death camps. Yet they continued to leave on transport trains. What else could they do? For the most part, they had no weapons. No training. And no way to fight the huge German army.

But Jews didn't just go meekly off to their deaths.

All along, from the very beginning of the ghettos, many Jews acted to save themselves and others. Some went into hiding. Thousands of young adults escaped from ghettos into nearby forests. They formed resistance groups to stop Nazi plans. They had few supplies and little food. But somehow, they destroyed Nazi rail lines. They blew up power stations.

Non-Jews resisted as well. One entire village in France, Le Chambon-sur-Lignon, hid five thousand people, more than half of them Jews.

In some instances, seeing what unspeakable things the Nazis were doing brought out the best in people.

Oskar Schindler was an unlikely hero. He had joined the Nazi Party in 1939 when he was thirty. He took advantage of anti-Jewish laws by buying a Jewish-owned factory in Poland. There, he used Jews from the

Oskar Schindler

nearby ghetto as forced laborers. But Schindler wound up saving those workers—more than a thousand Jews.

How did he do that? He used part of the factory to make weapons. The Jews in Schindler's factory seemed like they were doing work that helped the Nazis in the war. This may sound wrong. But these workers would not be sent off to death camps, because the Nazis needed them.

Plus, Schindler fooled officials. He gave them fake numbers for how many weapons his workers made. They actually made very few. At one point, Schindler's factory produced just one load of ammunition in about eight months.

What else did he do? Schindler drew up a list of workers' names and skills, changing ages and saying that doctors and lawyers were mechanics whose work was highly valued. Schindler spent all his money bribing SS officers, and buying his workers clothes, food, and medicine. He died in 1974, penniless and alone, but "his people," as he called them, brought his body to Israel to be honored and buried there.

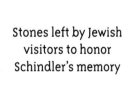

Stones left by Jewish visitors to honor Schindler's memory

One entire country stood up to Hitler. Although an occupied country under Hitler's control, Denmark refused to let the Nazis take its Jewish citizens. More than seven thousand Jews, along with non-Jewish family members, were smuggled in fishing boats to Sweden and safety.

There were revolts in concentration camps, even at killing centers. In Treblinka, prisoners seized weapons, set buildings on fire, and ran for their lives. About a hundred survived. At Auschwitz, prisoners blew up a furnace room.

The most famous story of resistance concerns the end of the Warsaw ghetto. By fall of 1942, only sixty-five thousand of the original half million Jews were still living there. The council chairman committed suicide in the summer, rather than write lists of people to be sent off and killed.

In January 1943, Nazi SS troops came through the gates to round up eight thousand people for death camps. However, a surprise was waiting for them. An army of Jews fought back. They were mostly young men and women. There weren't many, and they had few weapons and supplies. But they managed to kill many Germans. So the Nazi troops retreated.

Inside the Warsaw ghetto, more Jews joined the resistance, seven hundred in all. Young, old, men, women. They built hiding places. They linked sewer tunnels so people could move from place to place unseen. They made weapons.

Finally, on April 19, the Nazis came back. This time they had more soldiers, tanks, and machine guns.

Even so, the Jews refused to give up. The fighting lasted for four weeks. In the end, the Nazis burned every building to the ground. The ghetto fighters had nowhere to turn. Many died. Those captured were sent to the Treblinka death camp. Only a few dozen escaped. But the Warsaw ghetto uprising inspired others. It stood as a symbol of great courage against evil.

CHAPTER 10
Freedom!

Beginning in 1943, the tide of war turned against Germany. The Axis powers were fighting on too many fronts. And the Allies were coming at Hitler's army from every direction—north, south, east, west, and from the air.

US soldiers with
a Sherman tank

Did that stop or slow down the mass murder of Jews? No. In just one month in 1944, Germans sent 440,000 Jews from Hungary to their deaths.

As the Allies approached camps in Poland, the Nazis were determined to hide their crimes from the world. They tried to destroy camps and empty out prisoners. More than 150,000 prisoners were forced to march into Germany, farther from the Allied troops. Some traveled for miles and miles in bitter cold, without coats, boots, or any protection. Their only water came from falling snow. Thousands died along the way.

However, the Nazis did leave some prisoners behind. Russian soldiers found seven thousand inmates at Auschwitz. Though the Germans had destroyed much of the camp, several warehouses still stood. They were filled with prisoners' belongings: hundreds of thousands of men's suits and women's dresses that the Nazis had planned to sell. One warehouse held fourteen thousand pounds of human hair.

Finally free, some prisoners ran to greet the soldiers. Others felt afraid. They didn't want to come out because they didn't know what to expect.

As more and more camps were liberated, Allied troops couldn't take in the horror. The sick and starving. The dead bodies, stacked up like

logs. "Why do humans have to do this to other humans?" one American medic cried out.

The last camps were liberated in May 1945. Adolf Hitler was already dead. He'd committed suicide on April 30. His government had fallen apart. His dream of a Nazi empire lasting a thousand years was shattered.

On May 7, Germany officially surrendered.

The Holocaust was over.

CHAPTER 11
After

Italy had already surrendered to the Allies in 1943, and Japan signed a peace treaty in September 1945. World War II was over. About fifty-five million people had lost their lives—including civilians (people who weren't soldiers), Holocaust victims, and armed forces from both sides.

Top Nazis were brought to trial. They were accused of crimes against humanity. That means murder and other terrible acts directed against a whole population.

The first trials were held in Nuremberg, Germany, and lasted until 1949. Nazis faced judges from the United States, Great Britain, France, and the Soviet Union. Most were found guilty and either hanged or sent to prison.

A war crimes trial in Nuremberg

But many Nazis escaped from Germany to start new lives in other countries. For decades, "Nazi hunters" searched for these men and women. Over the years, some were brought to trial. One man, Adolf Eichmann, was caught in Argentina, tried in Israel in 1961, and executed. Adolf Eichmann's job was to carry out the plan for the Final Solution.

Adolf Eichmann on trial

Trials continued for decades. In 2016, prison guards and office workers were still facing court charges in Germany for war crimes. These people were in their nineties. One ninety-four-year-old witness, Leon Schwarzbaum, was a survivor of the

Leon Schwarzbaum

Holocaust. He told a reporter that punishment wasn't the only reason for a trial. It was to hear the truth.

But neither punishment nor the truth could change the past. Millions upon millions of people had been killed. Millions more had been uprooted. Forced from their homes and their countries.

After the war, people tried to return to countries that had been occupied. Some found their houses destroyed. Others found they weren't wanted. Violence against Jews continued. Where would these displaced persons—DPs—go?

The Allied military set up camps in Europe. In a way, the people there were still prisoners. Some lived in these camps for years. Gradually things were sorted out. Many Jews emigrated to Israel, a new Jewish homeland created in 1948. Some left for the United States and other countries.

Five years after the war, there were only forty-five thousand Jews left in Poland, down from more than three million. Germany, which had

started with half a million Jewish people, now had thirty-seven thousand. Austria's two hundred fifty thousand Jews were reduced to eighteen thousand.

For a time, survivors of the Holocaust kept silent. What they had gone through was too painful to talk about. But then they began to speak out. They didn't want people to forget the horror. If people didn't hear about the Holocaust, then history might repeat itself one day.

Museums and Memorials

Holocaust museums and memorial sites have been built around the world. In the United States, the national United States Holocaust Memorial Museum is in Washington, DC, but there are many other sites of remembrance from coast to coast.

United States Holocaust Memorial Museum

In Germany and Poland, concentration camps have been turned into museums. Survivors are fewer and fewer. Soon all will have died. But their stories must be passed on to future generations.

Yad Vashem: the World Holocaust Remembrance Center in Jerusalem, Israel

There were some German heroes in the Holocaust. They risked their lives hiding Jews, smuggling them to safety, supporting resistance. Still, as a whole, the German people kept silent. Camp employees. Secretaries who worked in Nazis' offices. Ordinary German citizens. Some who knew what was happening gave the excuse that they were only following orders. But how could they watch and say nothing? Had they agreed with Hitler's ideas about a master race of "Aryans"? Or were they afraid to speak up, in case they would be punished or killed?

Yet German soldiers who refused to kill did not receive harsh punishment from military or Nazi leaders. One group of German women protested when their Jewish husbands were rounded up by police and imprisoned. The men were freed and the couples were reunited.

Gerda Weissmann Klein spoke out about the Holocaust for decades. After the war, she and her husband moved to upstate New York. She raised a family, wrote books, and worked with schools to teach tolerance. She was awarded the Medal of Freedom in 2011 by President Barack Obama. That is the highest honor a US civilian can receive.

"Hatred and tyranny are not over," she declared.

What if more people had stood up to Hitler and the Nazis?

A Protestant minister in Germany admitted to once having been anti-Semitic. His name was Martin Niemöller. He had been a member of the Nazi Party. During the war, however, Niemöller changed. He saw the evil for what it was. He spent seven years in concentration camps for speaking out against Hitler.

In his speeches, Niemöller named groups of people who were taken away while he had remained silent. He included Jews, Communists, Catholics, and more. But he always ended with:

Martin Niemöller

Then they came for me—
And there was no one left to speak out for me.

Genocide

The word *genocide* was coined during the Holocaust. Its definition is: the deliberate killing of people from a particular group. Tragically, the mass killing of Jews by the Nazis is not the only instance of genocide. There have been others in much more recent times. Starting in 2003, in Sudan, a country in northeastern Africa, wild gangs sponsored by the government began slaughtering people who lived in an area called Darfur. Victims were killed because of their race, not their religion, with black Darfuri targeted. To date, more than four hundred thousand people have been killed and three million sent into exile.

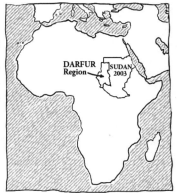

Timeline of the Holocaust

1933 — First anti-Jewish laws are passed

— First concentration camp, Dachau, is established for political prisoners

1934 — Hitler becomes führer

1938 — Violence against Jews sweeps across Germany and Austria during Kristallnacht, the "Night of Broken Glass"

1939 — Hitler invades Czechoslovakia and Poland

— World War II begins in Europe

1940 — Jewish ghettos in Lodz and Warsaw, Poland, are established and sealed

— The initial concentration camps in Auschwitz are built

1942 — Mass murders begin in Auschwitz and other killing centers

1943 — Hundreds of Jews fight against Nazis in the Warsaw ghetto uprising

1944 — First concentration camp is liberated by Russian soldiers

— Anne Frank and her family are arrested in Amsterdam

— In the winter, death marches from camps begin

1945 — Auschwitz is liberated

— Hitler commits suicide

— Germany and Japan surrender, and World War II ends

— Nuremberg trials against German war criminals begin

1953 — The first national Holocaust memorial, Yad Vashem, is established in Israel

Timeline of the World

1933 — Franklin D. Roosevelt is sworn in as the thirty-second US president

1938 — The ballpoint pen is first patented

— "War of the Worlds" radio broadcast of fictional alien invasion causes panic across the United States

1939 — Batman first appears in comic books

1940 — The oldest US freeway, the Pasadena Freeway, opens

— Color television is publicly demonstrated for the first time

1941 — New York Yankees win the World Series, their fifth championship out of the last six series

— Japan attacks Pearl Harbor, Hawaii, on December 7; the United States enters World War II

1943 — Italian dictator Benito Mussolini, allied with Hitler, is arrested by his government

— Rock-and-roll stars George Harrison (the Beatles) and Mick Jagger (the Rolling Stones) are born

1944 — Allied troops invade German-occupied France on June 6, D-Day

1945 — The United Nations is officially established

— Grand Rapids, Michigan, becomes the first community to add fluoride to their water to prevent cavities

1948 — The Jewish nation of Israel is established

1953 — Climbers Edmund Hillary and Tenzing Norgay are the first to reach the top of Mount Everest

Bibliography

*Books for young readers

*Abramson, Ann. *Who Was Anne Frank?* New York: Penguin Workshop, 2007.

Bergen, Doris L. *War and Genocide: A Concise History of the Holocaust*. Lanham, MD: Rowman and Littlefield Publishers, Inc., 2009.

Harran, Marilyn J. et al. *The Holocaust Chronicle: A History in Words and Pictures*. Lincolnwood, IL: Publications International, Ltd., 2003.

*Meltzer, Milton. *Never to Forget: The Jews of the Holocaust*. New York: HarperCollins Publishers, 1976.

Soumerai, Eve Nussbaum, and Carol D. Schulz. *Daily Life During the Holocaust*. Westport, CT: Greenwood Press, 1998.

*Zullo, Allan, and Mara Bovsun. *Survivors: True Stories of Children in the Holocaust*. New York: Scholastic Inc., 2004.

Website

The United States Holocaust Memorial Museum. www.ushmm.org